CORNERSTONE

Published by:
Cornerstone Publishing & Distribution, Inc.
(also HORIZON PUBLISHERS)
PO Box 490
Bountiful, UT 84011-0490
800-453-0812
www.horizonpublishers.com
Email: horizonp@burgoyne.com

First Printing: September, 1997

Printed in the United States of America
05 04 03 02 01 00   10 9

ISBN 0-88290-614-3

CONTENTS

1

EDITOR'S PREFACE

At Horizon Publishers, considerably more than a thousand manuscripts and query letters are received and processed each year. Many are on secular subjects and are considered for publication in the general book trade markets. About half of the communications received, however, are manuscripts and projects on religious topics intended for Latter-day Saint readers.

Out of the hundreds of manuscripts we receive which are intended for the LDS marketplace, we discover a unique few we feel are truly excellent contributions—they lift and inspire, they teach important principles in areas where confusion or misunderstandings may exist, they have the potential to touch and motivate many readers, and they make a fresh new contribution to the understanding of gospel principles. They're not trite rehashes of previously-covered concepts. They treat sacred teachings with reverent dignity. They are

2

OBSERVATIONS CONCERNING THE ENDOWMENT

MAINTAINING THE SACRED NATURE OF TEMPLE COVENANTS

This book is written for those who have previously attended the temple and have participated in the sacred endowment ordinance. Its objective is to provide them with keys of scriptural understanding which will help them expand their knowledge of sacred things and will lead them toward exaltation in our Heavenly Father's eternal kingdom.

It is not written to describe or depict sacred principles or procedures which, by covenant, endowed temple attenders have pledged not to discuss outside of the temple. Indeed, both the author and the editors strongly feel that such sacred information is not to be shared with those who are not worthy or who are as yet unprepared to enter the holy temple.

Everyone who receives the endowment solemnly covenants never to disclose certain things learned there as part of the endowment ceremony. This is because the endowment reveals some very sacred information—information that God intends people to learn only after they have shown that they intend to keep his commandments.

This book doesn't disclose any of that information. As the scriptures teach us, the Lord has secrets and covenants which he reveals only to the faithful: "The secret of the Lord is with them that fear him; and he will shew them his covenant." (Psalm 25:14) The covenants of non-disclosure taken by those who receive the endowment are in keeping with the spirit of this passage and are to be taken very seriously.

Elder Boyd K. Packer, in his inspirational book, *You may claim the blessings of The Holy Temple*, expresses the approach which has guided us in this matter:

> Our reluctance to speak of the sacred temple ordinances is not in any way an attempt to make them seem more mysterious or to encourage an improper curiosity about them. The ordinances and ceremonies of the temple are simple. They are beautiful. They are sacred. They are kept confidential lest they be given to those who are unprepared. Curiosity is not a preparation. Deep interest itself is not a preparation. Preparation for the ordinances includes preliminary steps: faith, repentance, baptism, confirmation, worthiness, a maturity and dignity worthy of one who comes

invited as a guest into the house of the Lord. (*The Holy Temple*, p. 26)

Unfortunately, there at times appears to be some variance of perspective among endowed individuals concerning just what is and is not appropriate to discuss about the temple and it sacred ceremonies. Some say those items which are to be held in strict confidence are clearly defined in the endowment ceremony itself, and that other items not thus excluded are appropriate for mention and comment in Church meetings and in other gatherings of the Saints as the Spirit leads and directs.

Others have opinions which are far more restrictive, sometimes to an extreme, attempting to hold as confidential information which has been published for general distribution by The Church of Jesus Christ of Latter-day Saints and/or discussed in public discourses by General Authorities.

Both groups have the same objectives: to lift and inspire the Saints, doing whatever is appropriate to lead them toward their salvation and exaltation. Both groups seek to obey the Lord's admonitions to "Trifle not with sacred things," (D & C 6:12) and to "Give not that which is holy unto the dogs, neither cast ye your pearls before swine, lest they trample them under their feet, and turn again and rend you" (Matthew 7:6). The two groups just differ in methods and approach.

As authors and publishers, and as faithful and endowed members of the Church, we have no desire to be involved in any dispute or criticism occasioned by this divergence of opinions. Therefore, we have elected to present any descriptions of the temple ceremony through published statements from such carefully scrutinized and authorized works as the *Encyclopedia of Mormonism*, or from various works published by the

Church or by its past or present General Authorities. The focus of this book is on the scriptural symbols which relate to the endowment, not on the ceremony itself. We seek to lift, teach, bless and inspire, not to be caught up in controversy and disputations.

MANY SOURCES OF INFORMATION ABOUT THE TEMPLE ARE AVAILABLE

Given the correct circumstances, however, there is much that appropriately can be said about the endowment outside the temple without violating those sacred covenants of non-disclosure. Resources produced both by the Church and by individuals closely associated with it discuss temple ceremonies in some detail and are readily available to members and non-members alike. A list of some of these items is provided in the "Additional Resources" section at the end of this book.

THE ENDOWMENT IS A RE-ENACTMENT OF SCRIPTURAL IMAGES AND SYMBOLS

The endowment can be understood in large part as a re-enactment of images and symbols which are already available in the scriptures. Recognizing those images, and understanding what they mean in the context of the scriptures, is an important step in understanding the endowment. Throughout this book, then, the endowment will be discussed in terms of the scriptural imagery in which it is grounded.

Remember this key concept about going to the temple: the endowment is a re-enactment of scriptural images and symbols. Understanding this concept will help prepare you to understand the many aspects of the scriptural symbols which are related to the endowment.

3

THE CENTRAL FOCUS OF THE ENDOWMENT

LEARNING CELESTIAL PASSWORDS

When the Saints laid the cornerstone for the Salt Lake Temple, Brigham Young gave an address explaining to the members in attendance, most of whom had not yet received the endowment, the significance of temple worship. In the course of that address, President Young gave the most succinct but informative description of the endowment yet written. It is often reproduced in Church publications. You can probably find it in your current Priesthood or Relief Society personal study guide. This is his definition:

> Your endowment is, to receive all those ordinances in the house of the Lord, which are necessary for you, after you have departed this life, to enable

you to walk back to the presence of the Father, passing the angels who stand as sentinels, being enabled to give them the key words, the signs and tokens, pertaining to the holy Priesthood, and gain your eternal exaltation in spite of earth and hell. (*Discourses of Brigham Young*, p. 416)

Note the image that President Young paints: after we have "departed from this life" (presumably, after we have been resurrected), we must physically "walk back" to God's presence. On the way, we will be met by guards, "angels who stand as sentinels." To pass these guards, we must show that we are authorized to live with God by presenting certain celestial passwords—what President Young calls "key words," "signs," and "tokens." Only after we have given these passwords and signs will the sentinels allow us into God's presence, where we will be exalted. The purpose of the endowment, President Young says, is to teach us those passwords.

Once we grasp this image, it becomes clear why the endowment is so important. Throughout the scriptures, and every time we receive a gospel ordinance such as baptism, God promises that he will allow the faithful to live in his presence. It is during the endowment that the faithful learn, at a very practical level, how to get there.

THE IMAGE OF PASSING ANGELIC SENTINELS

The image of passing an angelic guard to enter into God's presence is not President Young's alone; it is found in the scriptures as well. In Doctrine and Covenants 132:19, we read that those who keep the new and everlasting covenant of marriage will not only have their marriage in full force after the resurrection, but will also "pass by the angels, and the gods, which are set there, to their exaltation and glory in all things."

The image of the angelic sentinels contains an echo of the image of the cherubim with the flaming sword who guarded "the way of the tree of life" after Adam and Eve were driven from the Garden of Eden (Genesis 3:24). A shadow of the same image remains in the popular conception of St. Peter standing guard at the pearly gates.

THE USE OF SACRED "KEY WORDS"

The concept of sacred "key words" is also found in the scriptures. In figure 3 of *Facsimile 2*, in the *Book of Abraham*, we see a drawing of an Egyptian sun god surrounded by hieroglyphics. Joseph Smith explained that this image represents "God, sitting upon his throne . . . with a crown of eternal light on his head." Referring, presumably, to the hieroglyphics surrounding the sun god, Joseph went on to explain that the image also represents "the grand Key-words of the Holy Priesthood, as revealed to Adam in the Garden of Eden, as also to Seth, Noah, Melchizedek, Abraham, and all to whom the Priesthood was revealed."

It's not clear from context exactly whom Joseph means by "all to whom the Priesthood was revealed." Nor is it clear what it means for the priesthood to be "revealed." Does that mean being ordained to the priesthood? Or is Joseph Smith talking only about the great patriarchs and prophets to whom dispensations of the gospel were revealed after periods of apostasy? Or is he talking about yet something else?

REVELATION OCCURS
DURING THE ENDOWMENT

One thing, however, is clear: like Brigham Young, Joseph Smith taught that certain "Key-words of the Holy Priesthood" have been revealed to some people, and that the use of sacred key words dates all the way back to Adam and continued throughout the Old Testament dispensations.

Brigham Young taught that revelation occurs during the endowment; Joseph Smith's explanation of *Facsimile 2*, figure 3, may therefore be a reference to the endowment as well. If so, then we are to understand that receiving the endowment places us in company with Adam, Seth, Noah, Melchizedek, and Abraham: what was revealed to them is revealed to us as well.

The use of key words appears again in Doctrine and Covenants 130:11, where Joseph Smith explains the meaning of the white stone mentioned in Revelation 2:17. First, Joseph says that the white stone is a personal Urim and Thummim which each person in the celestial kingdom can use to learn about "things pertaining to a higher order of kingdoms." Joseph then says that

> a white stone is given to each of those who come into the celestial kingdom, whereon is a new name written, which no man knoweth save he that receiveth it. The new name is the key word.

The sentence structure here is somewhat ambiguous; it's not clear whether the white stone, with the key word written on it, is given to those who come into the celestial kingdom *when* they come into the celestial kingdom or some time *before*. In any case, we find here the same basic idea we found in Brigham Young's explanation of the endowment: those who enter the celestial kingdom need to be given certain celestial key words. Much of the endowment is structured around this idea. (There will be more said about the image of the white stone and the new name later.)

PROMISES ARE REQUIRED
BEFORE BLESSINGS ARE GRANTED

Over and over, the scriptures teach that before we can receive blessings from God, we must promise to keep his commandments. This promise is to be made formally; that is to say, it is to be made as a sacred covenant with God.

For example, before the Israelites entered the promised land, Moses had them covenant to obey God's law so that God could bless them. Every single person in the camp—men, women, children, even the Gentiles living with the Israelites—had to make this covenant. Moses explained that without the covenant, God *could not* fulfill his promise to bless the people. He said,

> Ye stand this day all of you before the LORD your God; your captains of your tribes, your elders, and your officers, with all the men of Israel,
> Your little ones, your wives, and thy stranger that is in thy camp, from the hewer of thy wood unto the drawer of thy water:
> That thou shouldst enter into covenant with the LORD thy God, and into his oath, which the LORD thy God maketh with thee this day:
> That he may establish thee to day for a people unto himself, and that he may be unto thee a God, as he hath said unto thee, and as he hath sworn unto thy fathers,

to Abraham, to Isaac, and to Jacob. (Deuteronomy 29:10-13)

Note the beginning of that last verse: *"that he may establish thee. . . ."* The grammar here sets up a dependent relationship: God's blessings depend on the people having first entered into the covenant. If the people did not enter the covenant, these verses imply, it would be impossible for God to bless them, no matter how much he wanted to.

COVENANTS ARE THE CHANNELS THROUGH WHICH BLESSINGS FLOW

It would seem that the covenant is the channel through which God's blessings flow to us. If we refuse to open the channel, God cannot (under the conditions he has established) transmit the blessings. We find this same teaching in Doctrine and Covenants 82:10: "I, the Lord, am bound when ye do what I say; but when ye do not what I say, ye have no promise."

THE IMAGE OF "BINDING GOD"

The image of human beings *binding* God is extraordinarily powerful; in fact, if God himself weren't the speaker in this passage, the image would be blasphemous. But it suggests again the mutual obligation involved in a covenant relationship: once we open our end of the channel, God is committed, and the blessings will inevitably flow to us. But when we don't open our end of the channel ("when ye do not what I say"), then there is no other means of receiving the blessings ("ye have no promise").

GOSPEL ORDINANCES
TAKE THE FORM OF A COVENANT

Baptism, the sacrament, priesthood ordination—in every case we make certain promises (e.g. to "keep his commandments which he has given them") in exchange for certain blessings (e.g., "that they may always have his Spirit to be with them"). The endowment is no different. As Brigham Young taught, the blessings we receive during the endowment are the signs, tokens, and key words we need to walk back to God's presence.

The *Encyclopedia of Mormonism* summarizes these sacred covenants in these words:

> During the Endowment, solemn covenants are made pertaining to truthfulness, purity, righteous service, and devotion. In this way, the temple is the locus of consecration to the teaching of the law and the prophets and to the ways of God and his Son. One does not assume such covenants lightly. Modern commandments relating to temple building have been addressed to those "who know their hearts are honest, and are broken, and their spirits contrite, and are willing to observe their covenants by sacrifice—yea, every sacrifice which I, the Lord, shall command" (D&C 97:8-9). As with Abraham of old, latter-day revelation says that to obtain "the keys of the kingdom of an endless life" one must be willing to sacrifice all earthly things (*TPJS*, p. 322). ("Temple Ordinances: Temple Endowment," *Volume 4, p. 1444)*

Before we can receive those blessings, however, we must make specific promises to obey God's laws. Elder James E. Talmage, in his book *The House of the Lord*, summarized these sacred and binding covenants:

The ordinances of the endowment embody certain obligations on the part of the individual, such as covenant and promise to observe the law of strict virtue and chastity, to be charitable, benevolent, tolerant and pure; to devote both talent and material means to the spread of truth and the uplifting of the race; to maintain devotion to the cause of truth; and to seek in every way to contribute to the great preparation that the earth may be made ready to receive her King,—the Lord Jesus Christ. With the taking of each covenant and the assuming of each obligation a promised blessing is pronounced, contingent upon the the faithful observance of the conditions.

No jot, iota, or tittle of the temple rites is otherwise than uplifting and sanctifying. In every detail the endowment ceremony contributes to covenants of morality of life, consecration of person to high ideals, devotion to truth, patriotism to nation, and allegiance to God. (*The House of the Lord*, page 100.)

As Elder John A. Widtsoe once observed, "Temple covenants give tests by which one's willingness and fitness for righteousness may be known." The making of these covenants is one of the most significant events in our life. It is the key to our exaltation in the eternal realms of our God and His Christ.

As you attend the temple, carefully memorize those covenants, and memorize the sacred tokens which will allow you to pass the guardian sentinels. To do so is to accomplish the central focus of the endowment.

4

AN ANCIENT CEREMONY RESTORED THROUGH JOSEPH SMITH

THE RESTORATION OF AN ANCIENT CEREMONY

Between 1841 and 1845, members of the Church in Illinois established five Masonic lodges. The Masons were an organization who performed rituals purportedly dating back to the time of Solomon's Temple, if not earlier (i.e., to the time of Enoch or even Adam. Over 1300 members, including Joseph Smith and other prominent Church leaders, became Master Masons.

During these rituals, which were kept secret from the public, the Masons made covenants; learned the importance of leading virtuous lives and serving others; received special signs, tokens, and keywords; and performed ceremonies incorporating elements of the priesthood as practiced under the Law of Moses.

According to early Church leaders, Joseph Smith taught that the Masonic rituals were incomplete remnants of an ancient ceremony revealed by God and then lost through apostasy. These early LDS leaders understood the endowment to be the restoration of that original ceremony.

Apparently, the ceremony was revealed to Joseph Smith after he inquired of the Lord about the status of the teachings he'd received as a Mason (see "Freemasonry and the Temple," *Encyclopedia of Mormonism,* Volume 2, pp. 528-29; also, "Similarity of Priesthood in Masonry," pp. 67-75).

The interesting account of Joseph Smith's first teaching of the endowment to various leaders of the Church is recorded in the *History of the Church,* Volume 5, pp. 1-2, under the date of Wednesday, May 4, 1842. Joseph wrote,

I spent the day in the upper part of the store, that is in my private office (so called because in that room I keep my sacred writings, translate ancient records, and receive revelations) and in my general business office (that is where the Masonic fraternity meet occasionally, for want of a better place) in council with General James Adams, of Springfield, Patriarch Hyrum Smith, Bishops Newel K. Whitney and George Miller, and President Brigham Young and Elders Heber C. Kimball and Willard Richards, *instructing them in the principles and order of the Priesthood, attending to washings, anoint-*

ings, endowments and the communication of keys pertaining to the Aaronic Priesthood, and so on to the highest order of the Melchizedek Priesthood, setting forth the order pertaining to the Ancient of Days, and *all those plans and principles by which any one is enabled to secure the fullness of those blessings which have been prepared for the Church of the First Born, and come up and abide in the presence of the Eloheim in the eternal worlds. In this council was instituted the ancient order of things for the first time in these last days.* And the communications I made to this council were of things spiritual, and to be received only by the spiritual minded: and *there was nothing made known to these men but what will be made known to all the Saints of the last days, so soon as they are prepared to receive,* and a proper place is prepared to communicate them, even to the weakest of the Saints; therefore let the Saints be diligent in building the Temple, and all houses which they have been, or shall hereafter be, commanded of God to build; and wait their time with patience in all meekness, faith, perseverance unto the end, *knowing assuredly that all these things referred to in this council are always governed by the principle of revelation.* [Emphasis added]

Joseph Smith gave the endowment to the Quorum of the Twelve, and also the keys of the sealing power, in March or early April of 1844, in Nauvoo. According to Elder Orson Hyde,

Before I went east on the 4th of April, last, we were in council with Brother Joseph almost every day for weeks. Says Brother Joseph, in one of those councils, "There is something going to happen; I don't know what it is, but the Lord bids me to hasten, and give you your endowment before the temple is finished." He conducted us through every ordinance of the holy priesthood, and when he had gone through with all the ordinances he rejoiced very much and said, "Now if they kill me you have got all the keys, and all the ordinances, and you can confer them upon others, and . . . on your shoulders will rest the responsibility of leading this people for the Lord is going to let me rest awhile. (Orson Hyde, *Millennial Star*, Vol. 5, p. 104, December, 1844. See *Temples of the Most High*, "The Beginning of Ceremonial Endowments in This Dispensation," pp. 283-86 for further information.)

Some gospel ordinances, e.g., baptism and the sacrament, follow a set script which has not changed (or has changed only very slightly) since ancient times. By contrast, the ceremony in which the endowment is presentcd (but not the endowment itself) has been modified several times just since it was revealed to Joseph Smith. This seems to be because this ceremony apparently is tailored by the Lord to the needs of particular cultures and times.

In the first modern revelation referring explicitly to the temple endowment, the Lord indicated that while the endowment might, in one sense, be continuous with ordinances revealed anciently (for example, to Adam, Seth, Noah, and the other patriarchs mentioned in *Facsimile 2*, figure 3, in the *Book of Abraham*), the ceremony revealed to Joseph Smith had been designed to meet the particular needs of Latter-day Saints:

> And verily I say unto you, let this house be built unto my name, that I may reveal mine ordinances therein unto my people;
> For I deign to reveal unto my church things which have been kept hid from before the foundation of the world, *things that pertain to the dispensation of the fullness*

of times. (Doctrine and Covenants 124:40-41; emphasis added)

Presumably, then, the ceremony revealed to Joseph had certain unique elements not to be found in the endowment ceremony from any previous dispensation. (See *Heber C. Kimball to Parley P. Pratt,* June 17, 1842, LDS Church Archives)

UNIQUE ELEMENTS FOR MODERN TIMES

By the same token, the endowment ceremony currently performed in temples has unique elements not to be found in Joseph Smith's endowment, or even in the endowment performed ten years ago. With the passage of time, the saints' needs and cultural understanding apparently have changed, and under the direction of the living prophets and apostles the endowment has changed with them. One of the most significant and innovative changes is that the ceremonial drama, which used to be presented by live actors, is now presented on film in almost all the temples. Other changes have followed.

Some of the most recent changes to the endowment, for instance (made in 1990), reflect our culture's increased emphasis on the equal partnership of spouses and our deepening respect for Christian churches with whom we formerly had rather hostile relations.

Other changes have made the ceremony briefer and simpler, and thus more accessible. Records indicate that early endowment sessions performed in the Nauvoo Temple lasted over five hours, as compared to current sessions which last about an hour and a half.

The endowment may continue to change in the future as we continue to progress as a people. With the Church's continued international growth, it would not be surprising if we eventually reached a point when slightly different versions of the endowment were authorized for use in different parts of the world. But this, of course, is only speculation.

It should be recognized that the changes which have occurred are in the ceremonial drama—the dramatic presentation which provides the teaching framework for the endowment experience. The most basic elements of the endowment—the covenants, signs, tokens, and key words—presumably will remain the same. But the images accompanying the presentation of those elements—presented in the ceremonial drama— have been and may continue to be modified so as to most effectively meet different cultures' needs and circumstances on their own terms.

GOD ADAPTS HIS WORDS
TO PARTICULAR NEEDS

As Nephi reminds us, God adapts his words to the particular needs and understanding of all his children. This principle is clearly seen in the ongoing development of the endowment.

> For my soul delighteth in plainness; for after this manner doth the Lord God work among the children of men. For the Lord God giveth light unto the understanding; for *he speaketh unto men according to their language, unto their understanding.* (2 Nephi 31:3)

5

ON-GOING PREPARATIONS FOR THE BLESSINGS OF THE ENDOWMENT

Preparation participating in the endowment is an ongoing process. How much you learn and receive during your temple attendance is dependent upon how carefully and continually you prepare yourself to be in tune and receptive.

KEEP THE COMMANDMENTS AND ENDOWMENT COVENANTS

The endowment can be understood as a blessing God reserves for those who keep his commandments.

This is why the scriptures insist that those who attend the temple must be worthy to do so, i.e., must be meeting a certain standard of faithfulness to God's laws.

The image the scriptures present is that we go to the temple (God's house) to meet God, to receive blessings from his hand, to learn his will, and to enjoy his presence. But if we go unworthily—if we ignore his commandments one day and then expect him to grace us with his presence and teachings the next—God will refuse to meet with us; and if we insist on staying in his house despite our unworthiness, he may leave, offended. The Lord has revealed that

> Inasmuch as my people build a house unto me in the name of the Lord, and do not suffer any unclean thing to come into it, that it be not defiled, my glory shall rest upon it;
> Yea, and *my presence shall be there, for I will come into it, and all the pure in heart that shall come into it shall see God.*
> *But if it be defiled I will not come into it, and my glory shall not be there; for I will not come into unholy temples.* (Doctrine and Covenants 97:15-17)

The standards for temple worthiness are the basic norms of conduct for members of the Church: pay your tithing, observe the Word of Wisdom, attend church regularly, magnify your calling, follow the prophet, keep the law of chastity. The questions for temple recommend interviews change slightly from time to time, but the basic idea remains the same: keep the commandments if you expect God to meet with you in his house.

But once you have obtained your own endowment, you have taken upon yourself a series of very profound covenants which should be guiding your day-by-day conduct. Memorize those covenants as you repeat them in future endowment sessions. Then ponder them carefully, and study the deepest implications of fulfilling them fully.

When you have internalized them, they have the power to shape your conduct throughout your life. They reach beyond the questions asked in temple recommend interviews. They penetrate to the core of how you will choose to live your life as you prepare to be worthy to receive the richest blessings of eternity.

Study the Endowment-related Portions of the Scriptures

God teaches us "line upon line, precept upon precept" (2 Nephi 28:30). Before we can fully understand what he teaches us during the endowment, we need to have some basic understanding of what he teaches us in the specific scriptures which relate to those same teachings in the endowment ceremony.

In particular, we need to understand the plan of salvation, especially as it is laid out in the creation narratives of the Books of Genesis, Moses, and Abraham. Study them!

We also need to be familiar with the symbolism of the Levitical priesthood, i.e., the priesthood as practiced under the Law of Moses, since much of the endowment's imagery enlarges upon that symbolism. It is these symbols which make the endowment stand out so markedly in comparison to worship in other Christian churches and even in contemporary Judaism.

Most Christians regard the Levitical priesthood as merely a type of Christ's atonement and therefore they retain its symbols in extremely muted form, if at all. While Latter-day Saints, too, regard the Levitical priesthood as a type of Christ, the endowment grants that priesthood additional status as a living tradition in its own right and consequently sets its symbols on center stage.

Quoting heavily from the scriptures, this book is intended to help you understand how those symbols of the Levitical Priesthood are at work in the endowment.

LEARN TO UNDERSTAND SYMBOLS THAT BOTH REVEAL AND CONCEAL

Symbolism was a mainstay of the teachings of Jesus. Matthew claims that Jesus never taught the multitudes without the use of symbols or figures. He wrote,

> All these things spake Jesus unto the multitude in parables; and without a parable spake he not unto them:
> That it might be fulfilled which was spoken by the prophet, saying, I will open my mouth in parables; I will utter things which have been kept secret from the foundation of the world. (Matthew 13:34-35)

Matthew also says that Jesus used figures deliberately to obscure his teachings, so that the multitude would not understand them. "It is given unto you," Jesus explained to his disciples, "to know the mysteries of the kingdom of heaven, but to them [the multitude] it is not given" (Matthew 13:11).

While the parables no doubt had this obscuring effect, it should be noted that the nature of figures is to both *reveal* and *conceal*. In other words, a figurative presentation not only obscures, at one level, the truth being presented, but simultaneously, at another level, it serves to help us understand the truth in a new way.

When Jesus describes missionary work in terms of a sower casting seed, for instance, he not only obscures, for some listeners, the fact that he is talking about missionary work, but he also helps us understand missionary work in a new way. The symbols used in the endowment serve the same purpose: they may serve to conceal the truth at one level, but they simultaneously reveal it to us in a new light at another level.

Learn to Recognize Both "Signifiers" and "Signifieds"

In linguistic jargon, a symbol has two parts: a *signifier* and a *signified*. The *signifier* is what we generally speak of as the symbol "itself"—the colored material that flies on a flagpole, or the pieces of broken bread on a sacrament tray. The *signified* is what we generally speak of as the meaning of the symbol—the country that the flag stands for, or the body of Christ represented by the bread.

The *signifier* is concrete; the *signified* is abstract. This is the power of using a symbol: a single concrete object is used to invoke a whole nebula of meaning. A flag stands not just for a country, but for that country's people, its history, its various aspirations and values, the dead who have fallen in defense of those values, the spirit of patriotism that preserves their memory, and so on. The broken bread stands not only for Christ's body, but for his atonement, his mercy, his compassion, his suffering, his mission, forgiveness, reconciliation, our willingness to keep his commandments, our discipleship, our communion with God and each other, and so on.

In short, symbols rarely have a single meaning. Signifiers and signifieds do not fall into neat one-on-one relationships. This means that almost every scriptural image used as a signifier in the endowment refers to not just one meaning, but to a complex web of meanings. It is this fact which makes the endowment such a rich experience—an experience in which an alert participant can continue to learn throughout his lifetime.

This book will merely begin to help you see the relationship between the endowment's signifiers and signifieds. The endowment will open up for you as you begin to grasp more of each symbol's various meanings and begin to see the complex interactions between those meanings, as well as their interaction with the meanings of other symbols. The most meaningful insights occur when you begin to see how events and aspects of your own life function as signifieds to the endowment's signifiers, i.e., how the endowment provides a symbolic representation of your daily life.

PRAY FOR UNDERSTANDING
OF SPECIFIC ELEMENTS OF THE ENDOWMENT

When Jesus visited the Nephites after his resurrection, he recognized that they were not yet fully prepared to understand his teachings. He therefore gave them the following counsel:

I perceive that ye are weak, that *ye cannot understand all my words* which I am commanded of the Father to speak unto you at this time.

Therefore, go ye unto your homes, and *ponder upon the things which I have said, and ask of the Father, in my name, that ye may understand,* and prepare your minds for the morrow, and I come unto you again. (3 Nephi 17:2-3)

As you prepare to understand or increase your understanding of the endowment, it is recommended that you follow the pattern Jesus outlines here: go home, ponder, and pray. Attend your church meetings, listen and learn, focusing especially on the plan of salvation. Then return home and ponder what you have been taught, using books like this to further prepare yourself to understand. Use, for instance, some of the excellent temple preparation resources produced by the Church for members' use at home.

Pray and Meditate While in the Temple

Finally, pray that God will help you begin to make sense of the endowment's vast web of intertwined meanings, particularly as those meanings touch your own life. Pray that you will gain deep, profound understanding of specific elements of the endowment. Each time you attend the temple, focus your efforts and preparation on understanding some specific new aspect of the endowment which you select under the guidance and tutoring of the Holy Spirit.

Two excellent times to do this are while you are in the temple chapel, waiting for your session to start, and while you are sitting in the celestial room after your session, reviewing what you have learned. Both are excellent times to come to God in fervent prayer, seeking additional understanding and enlightenment.

This profound pondering is meditation. Attending the temple provides a unique opportunity to combine the blessings of meditation with the blessings of the ennobling instructions communicated to us in the endowment presentation.

President David O. McKay wrote of this important combination of meditation and receiving instruction. His counsel was:

> I think we pay too little attention to the value of meditation, a principle of devotion. In our worship there are two elements: One is spiritual communion arising from our own meditation; the other, instruction from others, particularly from those who have authority to guide and instruct us. Of the two, the more profitable introspectively is the meditation. Meditation is the language of the soul. It is defined as "a form of private devotion, or spiritual exercise, consisting in deep, continued reflection on some religious theme." Meditation is a form of prayer. . . .
>
> Meditation is one of the most secret, most sacred doors through which we pass into the presence of the Lord. Jesus set the example for us. As soon as he was baptized and received the Father's approval, "This is my Beloved Son, in whom I am well pleased," Jesus repaired to what is now known as the mount of temptation. I like to think of it as the mount of *meditation* where, during the forty days of fasting, he communed with himself and his Father, and contemplated upon the responsibility of his great mission. (*Man May Know For Himself*, pp. 46-47)

6

A SYMBOLIC INITIATION INTO THE PRIESTHOOD

THE INITIATORY

The endowment ceremony has two separate parts. The first part is called the initiatory.

In terms of its imagery, the initiatory is patterned after the ceremony priests had to receive in Old Testament times before they were authorized to carry out priestly functions or enter the Tabernacle (later, the Temple). We read about this in *Exodus:*

> And this is the thing that thou [Moses] shalt do unto them [Aaron and his sons] to hallow them, to minister unto me in the priest's office:
>
> ... Aaron and his sons thou shalt bring unto the door of the tabernacle of the congregation, and shalt wash them with water.
>
> And thou shalt take the garments, and put upon Aaron the coat, and the robe of the ephod, and the ephod, and the breastplate, and gird him with the curious girdle of the ephod:
>
> And thou shalt put the mitre upon his head, and put the holy crown upon the mitre.
>
> Then shalt thou take the anointing oil, and pour it upon his head, and anoint him.
>
> And thou shalt bring his sons, and put coats upon them.
>
> And thou shalt gird them with girdles, Aaron and his sons, and put the bonnets upon them: and the priest's office shall be theirs for a perpetual statute: and thou shalt consecrate Aaron and his sons. (Exodus 29:1, 4-9)

Recall that Brigham Young taught that the purpose of the endowment is to reveal the signs, tokens, and key words "pertaining to the holy Priesthood." Consequently, priesthood imagery is fundamental to the endowment's symbolism, and the initiatory portion of the ceremony serves as a symbolic initiation into the priesthood.

Under the Law of Moses, only priests could enter the presence of God, who was understood to literally reside in the Tabernacle or Temple. As the Lord had said in Exodus 25:8, "Let them make me a sanctuary; that I may dwell among them." The Israelites took this idea so literally, in fact, that bells were sewn onto the high priest's robe so that when he went in "unto the holy place before the LORD," the LORD Jehovah would hear the bells ringing, recognize that it was the high priest approaching (rather than some unauthorized intruder), and allow him to enter without striking him dead (Exodus 28:33-35).

THE MEANING OF INITIATORY SYMBOLISM

The symbolic initiation into the priesthood which occurs during the endowment seems to draw on this Old Testament imagery. As has just been seen, Levitical priests were washed, anointed, and clothed in sacred "garments" so as to receive the authority to enter God's house and presence. Similarly, those who receive the initiatory today are symbolically washed, then anointed, and then clothed in temple garments to symbolize (1) that they are authorized to enter God's house, and (2) that the endowment they are about to receive authorizes them to someday walk back past the angelic sentinels into God's presence.

AN ENDOWMENT
IS A GIFT OF GOD'S POWER

The second part of the endowment ceremony is the ceremonial drama. It is the part people are usually referring to when they talk about "the endowment." It is in this portion of the endowment ordinance that one makes his sacred covenants and is rewarded for his pledging to be righteous by being taught how to pass by the guardian sentinels into God's exalted presence.

Literally, an endowment is a gift—a gift of God's power. When the words "endow" or "endowment" are used in the scriptures, they refer to gifts of power from

God. In the Gospel of Luke, for example, Jesus' final words to his disciples are an injunction to "tarry ye in the city of Jerusalem, until ye be endued with power from on high." (Luke 24:49)

These words are echoed in Doctrine and Covenants 105:11-12, where the Lord says that the redemption of Zion (following the saints' eviction from Jackson County, Missouri)

> cannot be brought to pass until mine elders are endowed with power from on high.
>
> For behold, I have prepared a great endowment and blessing to be poured out upon them, inasmuch as they are faithful and continue in humility before me.

The endowment to which these passages refer does not seem to be the temple ceremony which today has that same name. In Luke, Jesus is speaking of the gift of the Holy Ghost which the disciples are to receive at Pentecost. In Doctrine and Covenants 105, he is speaking of the keys and other blessings to be bestowed in the Kirtland Temple, several years before the ceremony known today as the endowment was revealed (see Doctrine and Covenants 110:9).

ENDOWMENT MEANS POWER FROM GOD AND IS ASSOCIATED WITH TEMPLES

In both cases, "endowment" means power from God and is associated with temples. In Luke 24:53, we are informed that while waiting for their promised endowment, the disciples "were continually in the temple, praising and blessing God." In the Doctrine and Covenants, the Lord commands the saints to build temples so that he can give them their promised endowment.

We are clearly meant to understand our temple endowment in terms of the same imagery: the endowment is a gift, received in the temple, which empowers us to return to God's presence and receive our exaltation. It is during this portion of the temple ceremony that we covenant to keep God's laws and receive in return the signs, tokens, and key words needed to walk back past the sentinels to his presence.

7

BEING PRONOUNCED
CLEAN BEFORE GOD

In this and the next three chapters, various aspects of the initiatory will be discussed. These are summarized in the *Encyclopedia of Mormonism* in this manner:

> Washings and anointings are preparatory or initiatory ordinances in the temple. They signify the cleansing and sanctifying power of Jesus Christ applied to the attributes of the person and to the hallowing of all life. They have biblical precedents. Women are set apart to administer the ordinances to women, and men are set apart to administer the ordinances to men. Latter-day Saints look forward to receiving these inspired and inspiring promises with the same fervent anticipation they bring to baptism. They come in the spirit of a scriptural command: "Cleanse your hands

and your feet before me" (D&C 88:74; *cf.* 1 John 2:27). A commemorative garment is given with these ordinances and is worn thereafter by the participant. ("Temple Ordinances: Washings and Anointings," *Encyclopedia of Mormonism*, Volume 4, p. 1444)

A Commandment to Cleanse Your Hands and Your Feet Before God

In a revelation to the saints in Kirtland, two-and-a-half years after the Church was restored, the Lord said:

> I give unto you, who are the first laborers in this last kingdom, a commandment that you assemble yourselves together, and organize yourselves, and prepare yourselves, and sanctify yourselves; yea, purify your hearts, and *cleanse your hands and your feet before me, that I may make you clean;*
>
> *That I may testify unto your Father, and your God, and my God, that you are clean from the blood of this wicked generation;* that I may fulfill this promise, this great and last promise, which I have made unto you [i.e., the promise that the saints shall someday see God], when I will. (Doctrine and Covenants 88:74-75)

It's not clear from the context whether the Lord intended that the saints were to meet together to literally cleanse their hands and feet. At the end of this same section, (verses 139-141) the Lord reveals the procedure for the ordinance of the washing of feet, which could be understood as a way of literally fulfilling the commandment quoted above; but that ordinance was used within the School of the Prophets and was never intended as a saving ordinance for all.

BEING PRONOUNCED CLEAN FROM THE BLOOD OF THIS WICKED GENERATION

But it is clear that before the saints can see God, the Lord must pronounce them "clean from the blood of this wicked generation." (See Doctrine and Covenants 88:75, 85, 138; 124:37) Today, that pronouncement is made during the initiatory, when representatives of the Lord ceremonially anoint each initiate with water and pronounce him or her clean from the blood of this wicked generation. The washing thus sets initiates apart from the world ("this wicked generation"), so that they enter a new relationship with God, a relation which ultimately will allow them to return to his presence.

THE WASHING IS ACCOMPANIED BY BLESSINGS TO EMPOWER RIGHTEOUS LIVING

Of course, in order to remain in this relationship, initiates must endure to the end in keeping God's commandments. The washing is, therefore, accompanied by a series of blessings to empower initiates to continue living in accordance with God's will. Since initiates are blessed with both physical well-being and moral strength, these blessings could be considered both temporal and spiritual. However, it might be more accurate to say that the blessings demonstrate the principle that God does not truly distinguish between the temporal and the spiritual: as he says in Doctrine and Covenants 29:34, "All things unto me are spiritual."

By blessing the physical body in order to empower initiates to live virtuous lives, the washing reminds us that because we are spirit beings inhabiting physical bodies, our physical and spiritual well-being are closely intertwined.

THE WASHING RECALLS CEREMONIAL WASHING FROM OLD AND NEW TESTAMENT TIMES

As mentioned earlier, the ordinance of washing recalls the ceremonial washing with water which priests had to undergo in Old Testament times before they were authorized to enter God's house and presence.

> And Aaron and his sons thou shalt bring unto the door of the tabernacle of the congregation, and shalt wash them with water. (Exodus 29:4)

During his ministry, Jesus used an ordinance of washing to symbolize the spiritual cleansing of his disciples and to indicate their oneness with him: "If I wash thee not," he told a protesting Peter, "thou hast no part with me" (John 13:8). Having "part with" Christ would suggest, among other things, being a joint-heir with him in God's kingdom, i.e., being exalted with him. (See Romans 8:17.) Similarly, in the revelation commanding the saints to build the Nauvoo Temple, the Lord names "washing" as one of the ordinances to be performed there (Doctrine and Covenants 124:39).

8

BEING CONSECRATED KINGS AND PRIESTS UNTO GOD

THE ANOINTING
IS A SYMBOL OF BEING CHOSEN
AND CONSECRATED BY GOD TO BE A RULER

As has been seen, priests in Old Testament times had to be anointed with oil before they were authorized to enter God's presence: "Then shalt thou take the anointing oil, and pour it upon his [Aaron's] head, and anoint him." (Exodus 29:7)

Kings were also anointed with oil, to indicate that they had been chosen and consecrated by God to serve as Israel's rulers. Hence Samuel anointed David to show that the Lord had rejected Saul and chosen a new ruler (even though it would be several years before the Israelites themselves would acknowledge David as the chosen ruler).

> And the Lord said unto Samuel, How long wilt thou mourn for Saul, seeing I have rejected him from reigning over Israel? fill thine horn with oil, and go, I will send thee to Jesse the Beth-lehemite: for I have provided me a king among his sons.
> . . . I will shew thee what thou shalt do: and thou shalt anoint unto me him whom I name unto thee.
> . . . And he [Jesse] sent, and brought him [David] in. Now he was ruddy, and withal of a beautiful countenance, and goodly to look to. And the Lord said, Arise, anoint him: for this is he.
> Then Samuel took the horn of oil, and anointed him in the midst of his brethren: and the Spirit of the Lord came upon David from that day forward. (1 Samuel 16:1, 3, 12-13)

Note that David's anointing is accompanied by an endowment of the Spirit, which seems to be understood here as divine power.

BECOMING KINGS AND PRIESTS UNTO GOD

At the beginning of the *Book of Revelation*, John describes Christ's atonement in terms of a symbolic washing and anointing, whereby the saints become "kings and priests unto God":

> [Grace be unto you] from Jesus Christ, who is the faithful witness, and the first begotten of the dead, and the prince of the kings of the earth. Unto him

that loved us, and washed us from our sins in his own blood,

And hath made us kings and priests unto God and his Father; to him be glory and dominion for ever and ever. Amen. (Revelation 1:5-6)

This image is quite complex and contains several possible meanings. By describing the saints as having been anointed "kings . . . unto God," John foreshadows the promise made by Christ later in Revelation that the faithful will rule with him in God's kingdom: "To him that overcometh will I grant to sit with me in my throne, even as I also overcame, and am set down with my Father in his throne." (Revelation 3:21)

Addressed to an infant Christian Church, still preoccupied with defining itself in opposition to Judaism, John's description of the saints as anointed kings may also be meant to convey the assurance that Christians, not Jews, are God's chosen "rulers in Israel," just as David, not Saul, became God's chosen ruler after Saul proved unfaithful.

THE ANOINTING IS A SYMBOL OF OBLIGATIONS AND PROMISES

By describing the saints as having been anointed "priests unto God," John invokes the image of priest as the one authorized to enter God's presence, thus reminding his readers that Christ's atonement makes it possible for them to "have right to . . . enter in through the gates" of the celestial kingdom (Revelation 22:14). The image is likely also meant as a reminder of the saints' role as God's servants and representatives to the world, a recurring theme in Revelation.

In short, when John speaks of the saints as having been washed and anointed "kings and priests unto God," he is reminding them (1) of their obligation to carry out God's work, and (2) the promise that if they are faithful, they will be exalted through Christ's atonement.

Whether John is speaking purely in figure or is alluding to an ordinance of anointing actually practiced by early Christians is unclear from the context. In both the Roman Catholic and Greek Orthodox churches, anointing is included as part of the baptismal rite since, according to tradition, anointing was an initiatory ordinance practiced in the primitive Church. John may well, then, be speaking literally.

In today's initiatory, at any rate, initiates are literally anointed to become kings and priests, or queens and priestesses, unto God. Obviously, the anointing performed during the initiatory involves the same symbolism as the anointing mentioned by John. That is to say, the anointing reminds initiates of their obligation to carry out God's work in this life, with the promise that if they are faithful, they will be exalted so they can continue to carry out God's work (i.e., direct his kingdom) in the next life.

The anointing is performed to empower initiates to endure to the end and thus prove worthy of exaltation. As a promise of exaltation in God's kingdom (albeit a conditional one), the anointing is an extremely important ordinance. In fact, "anointing" is the very first item on the list of temple ordinances given in Doctrine and Covenants 124:39.

9

RECEIVING A
PROTECTIVE SHIELD

OLD TESTAMENT PRIESTS WORE SPECIAL
CLOTHING TO ENSURE MODESTY

Following the pattern of Aaron's initiatory in Exodus 29 (washing, anointing, clothing), today's initiatory concludes with the clothing of initiates in the temple garment. The term "garment," of course, simply means an article of clothing and is used as such throughout the scriptures. Nowhere in either the King James Version of the Bible or the contemporary LDS Standard Works is the word "garment" used to refer explicitly to the particular piece of clothing we call the temple garment.

We do learn, however, that priests under the Law of Moses were required to wear a piece of clothing which sounds something like a modern temple garment:

And thou [Moses] shalt make them [the priests] linen breeches to cover their nakedness; from the loins even unto the thighs they shall reach:

And they shall be upon Aaron, and upon his sons, when they come in unto the tabernacle of the congregation, or when they come near unto the altar to minister in the holy place; that they bear not iniquity and die: it shall be a statute forever unto him and his seed after him. (Exodus 28:42-43)

Like a modern temple garment, these under-breeches extended some distance down the thigh and were worn "to cover" the wearer's "nakedness" (i.e., to ensure modesty). The priests, however, wore these breeches only while ministering at the Tabernacle; today a temple garment is worn at all times.

The *Encyclopedia of Mormonism* describes the temple garment initiates receive during the initiatory portion of the endowment ordinance in this manner:

Scripture . . . points toward the significance of sacral clothing. A biblical tradition teaches that Adam and Eve, prior to their expulsion from Eden, wore sacred clothing. "Unto Adam also and to his wife did the Lord God make coats of skins, and clothed them" (Gen. 3:21). These were given in a context of repentance and forgiveness, and of offering sacrifice and making covenants . . . .

The word "garment" has distinctive meanings to Latter-day Saints. The white undergarment worn by those members who have received the ordinance of the temple Endowment is a ceremonial one. All adults who enter the temple are required to wear it. In LDS temples, men and women who receive priesthood ordinances wear this undergarment and other priestly robes. The garment is worn at all times, but the robes are worn only in the temple. Having made covenants of righteousness, the members wear the garment under their regular clothing for the rest of their lives, day and night, partially to remind them of the sacred covenants they have made with God.

The white garment symbolizes purity and helps assure modesty, respect for the attributes of God, and, to the degree it is honored, a token of what Paul regarded as taking upon one the whole armor of God (Eph. 6:13; cf. D&C 27:15). It is an outward expression of an inward covenant, and symbolizes Christlike attributes in one's mission in life. Garments bear several simple marks of orientation toward the gospel principles of obedience, truth, life, and discipleship in Christ. ("Garments," *Encyclopedia of Mormonism*, Volume 2, p. 534)

THE IMAGE OF GOD GIVING SPECIAL CLOTHING TO THE FAITHFUL

The temple garment re-enacts an image which recurs throughout the scriptures: that of God giving special clothing to the faithful. In the Book of Revelation, for example, the Lord promises that the faithful members of the church in Sardis will be "clothed in white raiment."

Thou hast a few names even in Sardis which have not defiled their garments; and they shall walk with me in white: for they are worthy.

He that overcometh, the same shall be clothed in white raiment; and I will not blot out his name out of the book of life, but I will confess his name before my Father, and before his angels. (Revelation 3:4-5)

THE IMAGES OF DEFILED GARMENTS AND WHITE CLOTHING

Note that the image of clothing is actually used in this passage two different ways. First, defiling one's garments (literally, getting one's clothes dirty) is used as a symbol of unfaithfulness or sin. Second, wearing white clothing is a symbol of faithfulness and salvation. Those who are given white clothing to wear (at a literal level, those who have proven they can keep their clothes clean and can thus be trusted to wear white without staining the cloth) are also those whose names are recorded in the book of life and whom Christ confesses before the Father and his angels. In other words, they are those who enter the celestial kingdom.

DONNING TEMPLE GARMENTS IS A CEREMONIAL PRE-ENACTMENT OF GOD'S GIVING WHITE RAIMENT TO THE FAITHFUL

Clothing initiates in the temple garment is a ceremonial re-enactment (or perhaps more accurately, a *pre-enactment*) of God's giving "white raiment" to the faithful, and thus it serves as yet another symbol of the promise of exaltation.

THE IMAGES OF NAKEDNESS AND WEARING THE ROBE OF RIGHTEOUSNESS

A variation on the clothing image can be found in 2 Nephi 9:14:

Wherefore, we shall have a perfect knowledge of all our guilt, and our uncleanness, and our nakedness; and the righteous shall have a perfect knowledge of their enjoyment, and their righteousness, being clothed with purity, yea, even with the robe of righteousness.

In this version of the image, there are no dirty clothes: one wears either the "robe of righteousness" or nothing at all. Nakedness thus symbolizes "guilt" and "uncleanness," while to cover one's nakedness means to be absolved of guilt and made clean through Christ's atonement. The wearing of the temple garment symbolizes this too—the garment covers not only our physical nakedness, but our spiritual nakedness as well.

After Adam and Eve transgressed, they attempted to cover their nakedness with fig-leaf aprons (Moses 4:13). In light of 2 Nephi 9:14, we can read this action as a symbol of people's attempts to hide their guilt when they sin.

THE IMAGE OF COVERING OVER GUILT THROUGH CHRIST'S ATONEMENT

After Adam and Eve confessed their transgression, the Lord made coats of skin to cover their nakedness instead. Again in light of 2 Nephi 9:14, this could be read as a symbol of the true "covering over" of guilt which Christ's atonement provides when we repent; the animal which God presumably killed in order to make the coats of skin could be read as a symbol of Christ.

Again, the temple garment draws on all this symbolism. Wearing it reminds us that our sins have been forgiven through Christ's Atonement and that we should act accordingly.

GOD PROVIDES PHYSICAL REMINDERS
OF COVENANTS MADE

When God makes covenants with people in the scriptures, he often leaves a physical reminder of the covenant. Hence Israelites were required to circumcise themselves as a token of God's covenant with Abraham (Genesis 17:9-11). Later, they were commanded to hold a yearly Passover celebration to commemorate their deliverance from Egypt and thus remind themselves to keep the Lord's law (Exodus 13:6-9). Jesus instituted the sacrament as a regular reminder of the new covenant made possible by his Atonement (Matthew 26:26-28). Similarly, the constant wearing of the temple garment serves as a reminder of the covenants we make during the endowment.

SYMBOLS REMIND US OF COMMITMENTS
TO RIGHTEOUS CONDUCT

Special marks on the temple garment remind us to keep our covenants exactly and honorably, to control our thoughts and actions, to keep our bodies and spirits healthy, and to prepare for the Lord's Second Coming. In addition, wearing the garment reminds us that God has called us to do his work.

THE GARMENT IS A PROTECTIVE SHIELD

If we do what the garment reminds us of, God promises to protect us from Satan's power. This promise is a tremendous and tangible blessing that those who have received their endowment can enjoy throughout their lives.

10

A SIGNIFICANT AND SACRED KEY

GOD-GIVEN NAMES
SIGNIFY A NEW RELATIONSHIP WITH HIM

In the scriptures, particularly in the Bible, the Lord gives some people new names to symbolize their having entered a new relationship with him, and thus having undergone a change in their identity. Often, the giving of a new name is associated with the making of a covenant. When God covenanted to make Abram a "father of many nations," he changed Abram's name to Abraham in token of the new promise (Genesis 17:4-5). Similarly, when God reconfirmed the Abrahamic covenant to Jacob, he changed Jacob's name to Israel (Genesis 35:10-12). Though not in connection with a particular covenant, Jesus changed Simon's name to Peter to symbolize the new role he would someday assume as leader of the church (Matthew 16:17-19).

ZION SHALL BE CALLED BY A NEW NAME IN THE LAST DAYS

Isaiah uses the image of God's giving his people a new name to describe the redemption of Zion in the last days.

> For Zion's sake will I not hold my peace, and for Jerusalem's sake I will not rest, until the righteousness thereof go forth as brightness, and the salvation thereof as a lamp that burneth.
>
> And the Gentiles shall see thy righteousness, and all kings thy glory: and thou shalt be called by a new name, which the mouth of the Lord shall name. (Isaiah 62:1-2)

A NEW NAME WILL BE GIVEN TO THOSE ALLOWED TO ENTER THE CELESTIAL KINGDOM

In the *Book of Revelation*, this image is applied to those who are allowed to enter the heavenly Jerusalem, i.e., the celestial kingdom.

> Him that overcometh will I make a pillar in the temple of my God, and he shall no more go out: and I will write upon him the name of my God, and the name of the city of my God, which is new Jerusalem, which cometh down out of heaven from my God: and I will write upon him my new name. (Revelation 3:12)

Like the new names given to Abram, Jacob, Simon, and (according to Isaiah) the city of Zion, this new name seems to symbolize the redeemed's new relationship with God. As Paul would say, the old man of sin has been redeemed, reborn, and thus renamed as well. The new name is also associated, in Revelation, with the redeemed's permission to enter the celestial kingdom.

THE NEW NAME
IS A SYMBOL OF MERITING ETERNAL LIFE

Another reference to the new name occurs in Revelation 2:17. The opening line, "He that hath an ear, let him ear," is meant to alert readers that John is speaking in symbolic terms.

> He that hath an ear, let him hear what the Spirit saith unto the churches; To him that overcometh will I give to eat of the hidden manna, and will give him a white stone, and in the stone a new name written, which no man knoweth saving he that receiveth it.

In context, the hidden manna, the white stone, and the new name would all seem to be symbols drawn from Old Testament imagery of eternal life. This is how they are generally understood by Biblical commentators. Joseph Smith taught, though, that the white stone and the new name can be understood literally as well.

> Then [when the earth becomes the celestial kingdom] the white stone mentioned in Revelation 2:17, will become a Urim and Thummim to each individual who receives one, whereby things pertaining to a higher order of kingdoms will be made known;

And a white stone is given to each of those who come into the celestial kingdom, whereon is a new name written, which no man knoweth save he that receiveth it. The new name is the key word. (Doctrine and Covenants 130:10-11)

The New Name Is a Key Word

As the Lord explained it to Joseph, the new name is a key word given to those who enter the celestial kingdom. At this point, we have made our way full circle back to the signs, tokens, and key words which Brigham Young said we learn during the endowment.

Thus we are to understand that as part of the initiatory, members of the Church receive a new name which (1) symbolizes the new covenant relationship with God which they are entering through the endowment, and (2) serves as one of the key words needed to walk back to God's presence.

The Sacred and Confidential Nature of the New Name

Obviously, this new name is extraordinarily sacred; it is therefore used only in the temple while we are here in mortality.

11

THE
CEREMONIAL DRAMA

The second part of the endowment, following the
initiatory, is a sacred ceremonial drama beginning
with the Creation of the earth and ending with
our future return to God's presence. The drama explains
why we are living on earth and what we need to do to
prepare to enter the celestial kingdom.

THE PEDAGOGY OF THE TEMPLE SERVICE

Dr. John A. Widtsoe, a member of the Quorum of the
Twelve and a renowned teacher, made these profound
observations concerning the endowment ceremony
being a powerful teaching methodology:

> The temple ordinances encompass the whole plan
> of salvation, as taught from time to time by the leaders

of the Church, and elucidate matters difficult of understanding. . . . Moreover, this completeness of survey and expounding of the Gospel plan, makes temple worship one of the most effective methods in refreshing the memory concerning the whole structure of the gospel. . . .

The endowment and the temple work as revealed by the Lord to the Prophet Joseph Smith fall clearly into four distinct parts: the preparatory ordinances; the giving of instruction by lectures and representations; covenants; and, finally, tests of knowledge. . . .

We go to the temple to be informed and directed, to be built up and to be blessed. How is all this accomplished? First by the spoken word, through the lectures and conversations, just as we do in the class room, except with more elaborate care, then by the appeal to the eye by representations by living, moving beings; and by pictorial representations [and, we would now add, filmed presentations] in the wonderfully decorated rooms. . . . Meanwhile the recipients themselves, the candidates for blessings, engage actively in the temple service. . . . Altogether our temple worship follows a most excellent pedagogical system. ("Temple Worship," *The Utah Genealogical and Historical Magazine*, Volume 12, pp. 58- 59, April 1921, as cited in *The Holy Temple*; pp. 37-39).

PROPHETS WERE SHOWN CEREMONIAL DRAMAS TO HELP THEM UNDERSTAND GOD'S PLAN

According to the scriptures, some prophets were shown symbolic dramas in visions to help them understand God's plan for mankind. These dramas include Daniel's vision of the four beasts and the Messiah's final victory (Daniel chapters 7-8); Zechariah's series of symbolic Messianic visions (Zechariah chapters 3-6); John's vision of the history and future of the world recorded in the Book of Revelation (Revelation chapters 4-22); and Lehi's vision of the tree of life (1 Nephi 8).

Typically, in these dramas, the prophets are not only spectators, but also participants. Lehi, for example, is a central character in his own vision, and John is required at one point to take part in the symbolic drama of the Book of Revelation by eating a little book one of the angels in the drama is holding (Revelation 10:8-10). Likewise, in the ceremonial drama of the endowment, initiates are participants as well as spectators.

THE ENDOWMENT DEPICTS MAN'S PROGRESSION FROM THE CREATION TO EXALTATION

The drama depicts the eternal progression of Adam and Eve, from creation to exaltation. Adam and Eve are understood to represent all men and women, which is to say that what Adam and Eve must do to return to God's presence, we all must do as well. To symbolize this connection and to become participants in the drama rather than mere spectators, initiates repeat certain symbolic actions performed by the actors playing Adam and Eve.

DONNING CEREMONIAL CLOTHING RESEMBLING OLD TESTAMENT PRIESTS

During the drama, initiates don ceremonial clothing which resembles the clothing worn by priests who functioned under the Law of Moses. The *Book of Exodus* describes several articles of clothing which the priests were to wear:

And thou shalt take the garments, and put upon
Aaron the coat, and the robe of the ephod, and the
ephod, and the breastplate, and gird him with the curious girdle of the ephod:

And thou shalt put the mitre upon his head, and
put the holy crown upon the mitre. (Exodus 29:5-6)

Assuming that the items of clothing are listed in the
order in which they were donned, the coat (also trans-
lated as "tunic") would seem to be a basic garment over
which was worn the robe. The ephod has been
described as a "linen apron" worn over the robe (*New
International Version Bible*, p. 963). The breastplate, worn
only by the high priest, bore twelve stones representing
the tribes of Israel. The "curious girdle" was a type of
sash; the mitre, a type of cap. The "holy crown" was a
gold plate bearing the inscription, "Holiness to the
Lord" (Exodus 28:36), also worn only by the high priest.
Of these seven items of clothing, participants in the
modern endowment ceremony wear four.

PRIESTLY CLOTHING SYMBOLIZES AUTHORIZATION TO ENTER INTO GOD'S PRESENCE

Like the washing and anointing which are patterned
after the initiatory ceremony for Levitical priests, the
wearing of priestly clothing symbolizes the fact that initiates, like Levitical priests, are authorized to enter
God's house and are in the process of receiving the
authority to enter his presence.

The clothing also serves as a reminder that initiates
have been anointed to become priests and priestesses
unto God, with all that symbolizes.

12

THE CREATION

The endowment's ceremonial drama has several parts, representing the different stages of our eternal progression. These parts, for which related materials are presented in chapters 12 through 17 of this book, are summarized in the *Encyclopedia of Mormonism*, which tells us there is

> . . . a course of instruction by lectures and representations. These include a recital of the most prominent events of the Creation, a figurative depiction of the advent of Adam and Eve and of every man and every woman, the entry of Adam and Eve into the Garden of Eden, the consequent expulsion from the garden, their condition in the world, and their receiving of the Plan of Salvation leading to the return to the presence of God (Talmage, pp. 83-84). The Endowment instructions utilize every human faculty so that the meaning of the gospel my be clarified through art, drama, and

symbols. All participants wear white temple robes symbolizing purity and the equality of all persons before God the Father and his Son Jesus Christ. The temple becomes a house of revelation whereby one is instructed more perfectly "in theory, in principle, and in doctrine" (D&C 97:14). "This completeness of survey and expounding of the gospel plan makes temple worship one of the most effective methods of refreshing the memory concerning the entire structure of the gospel" (Widtsoe, 1986, p. 5). . . .

Participants in white temple clothing assemble in ordinance rooms to receive this instruction and participate in the unfolding drama of the Plan of Salvation. They are taught of premortal life; the spiritual and temporal creation; the advent of Adam and Eve, and their transgression and expulsion into the harsh contrasts of the mortal probation; the laws and ordinances required for reconciliation through the Atonement of Christ; and a return to the presence of God. The Endowment is a series of symbols of these vast spiritual realities, to be received only by the committed and spiritual-minded. ("Endowment," *Encyclopedia of Mormonism*, Volume 2, p. 455 and "Temple Ordinances," Volume 4, p. 1444)

GOD THE FATHER COMMANDED HIS SPIRIT CHILDREN TO CREATE THE EARTH

We learn from modern revelation that God the Father (who in the temple is called "Elohim," a Hebrew word for "God") did not create the world single-handedly. In fact, in a certain sense, it is inaccurate to say that the Father created the world at all. Rather, it was created at his command by some of his spirit children. This we learn from the Book of Abraham:

Now the Lord had shown unto me, Abraham, the intelligences that were organized before the world was; and among all these there were many of the noble and great ones;

And God saw these souls that they were good, and he stood in the midst of them, and he said: These I will make my rulers; for he stood among those that were spirits, and he saw that they were good. . .

And there stood one among them that was like unto God, and he said unto those who were with him: We will go down, for there is space there, and we will take of these materials, and we will make an earth whereon these may dwell: . . . (Abraham 3:22-24)

THE FATHER CREATED THE EARTH
BY HIS SON JEHOVAH

It is reasonable to assume that the spirit "that was like unto God" is God the Son (Jehovah, who is Jesus Christ), through whom, according to the *Book of Moses*, the Father created the heaven and the earth:

And it came to pass that the Lord spake unto Moses, saying: Behold, I reveal unto you concerning this heaven, and this earth; write the words which I speak. I am the Beginning and the End, the Almighty God; by mine Only Begotten I created these things . . . . (Moses 2:1)

Presumably, the other spirits mentioned in Abraham 3:24, whom the Son invites to help create the earth, are "the Gods" whom the Book of Abraham credits with the Creation (chapters 4-5). One of those "Gods" was Adam, who we learn from the Doctrine and Covenants is also called Michael (see Doctrine and Covenants 27:11 and 107:54).

Acting under the direction of the Father, the Gods created the earth in six stages, followed by a period of rest. These six stages, and the significant events which preceded them, can be studied by reading and comparing Genesis 1-2, Moses 1-3, and Abraham 3-5. You will gain much knowledge and understanding of the plan of salvation and of the endowment by giving them careful and repeated study and meditation.

THE FATHER AND SON TOGETHER CREATED MAN AND THEN WOMAN

In the final stage of creation before the period of rest, the Father himself descended with the Son to create human beings.

> And I, God, said unto mine Only Begotten, which was with me from the beginning: Let us make man in our image, after our likeness; and it was so . . . (Moses 2:26)

First the Father and the Son created a man's body and placed Adam's (Michael's) spirit into it. Like the rest of us, Adam could no longer remember his premortal life, including his involvement in the Creation, once he entered his mortal body. Then the Father and the Son created a woman so that Adam would have a suitable companion:

> And I, the Lord God, said unto mine Only Begotten, that it was not good that the man should be alone; wherefore I will make an help meet for him. (Moses 3:18)

13

EVENTS IN THE GARDEN OF EDEN

ADAM AND EVE WERE GIVEN AGENCY AND A PROHIBITION

When Adam and Eve were placed in the Garden of Eden, they were told that they could eat from every tree in the Garden, but that if they chose to eat the fruit of the Tree of Knowledge of Good and Evil, they would die.

And I, the Lord God, commanded the man, saying: Of every tree of the garden thou mayest freely eat,

But of the tree of the knowledge of good and evil, thou shalt not eat of it, nevertheless, thou mayest choose for thyself, for it is given unto thee; but, remember that I forbid it, for in the day thou eatest thereof thou shalt surely die. (Moses 3:16-17)

Since Latter-day Saints believe, on the basis of modern revelation, that it was necessary for Adam and Eve to fall, the Father's explicit prohibition "remember that I forbid it" remains something of a mystery. The prohibition is qualified somewhat in the Moses account, as compared to the Genesis account, by the addition of the words "nevertheless, thou mayest choose for thyself, for it is given unto thee." But the terms of prohibition still remain: "I forbid it." The added words seem to function simply as a recognition that regardless of what the Father forbids or allows, Adam and Eve still had their free agency and thus were capable of violating the Father's prohibition if they so chose.

DISREGARDING THE PROHIBITION SET THE PLAN IN MOTION

Why the Father would forbid Adam and Eve to do that which the plan of salvation hinged upon their doing remains unclear, though of course everyone has their favorite theory to explain the apparent contradiction.

My favorite theory, for what it's worth, is that the prohibition was merely temporary, and that eventually the Father would have commanded Adam and Eve to eat the fruit. By disregarding the prohibition, Adam and Eve set the plan in motion early, though the Father, of course, had foreseen that they would do so.

SATAN SOUGHT TO TEMPT AND BEGUILE EVE

In any case, Satan appeared in the Garden, once Adam and Eve had been left alone, to tempt them to disobey Father's prohibition. We learn from the Moses account that Satan (also called Lucifer) told Eve that eating the fruit would give her knowledge of good and evil, which in turn would make her like the Gods (Moses 4:11).

In other words, Satan gave Eve a partial explanation of the plan of salvation while trying to mislead and beguile her (Moses 4:6) by not telling her other pertinent information. He wanted her to become mortal so he could gain power over her. He did not explain to Eve that she would have to pass through a mortal existence where there is "opposition in all things" (2 Nephi 2:11) in order to be exalted to Godhood. He also did not tell her of the physical and spiritual death which would also result from the Fall and which would need to be atoned. He only told her, "Ye shall not surely die" (Moses 4:10).

Yet on the basis of this partial explanation of the plan of salvation given by Lucifer, Eve still recognized the necessity of bringing about the Fall and the good to be gained by it. She chose, therefore, to eat the forbidden fruit:

> And when the woman saw that the tree was . . . to be desired to make her wise, she took of the fruit thereof, and did eat, and also gave unto her husband with her, and he did eat.
>
> . . . And Eve . . . was glad, saying: Were it not for our transgression we never should have had seed, and never should have known good and evil, and the joy of our redemption, and the eternal life which God giveth unto all the obedient. (Moses 4:12; 5:11)

ADAM'S DESIRE
THAT THEY OBEY THE COMMAND
TO MULTIPLY AND REPLENISH THE EARTH

Lehi tells us that Adam's motivation for eating the forbidden fruit was somewhat different than Eve's. While Eve recognized the necessity of eating the fruit in order to gain knowledge of good and evil, Adam recognized the necessity of eating the fruit in order for them to remain together, and for them to be able to carry out the Father's command to multiply and replenish the earth. Hence Lehi says, "Adam fell that men might be . . . ." (2 Nephi 2:25)

It should be noted that according to both the Genesis and Moses accounts, Eve gave the fruit to Adam, which implies that she convinced him of the importance of eating it. Later, in a rather ignominious lapse, Adam used this fact to try to absolve himself of responsibility, protesting, "*She* gave me of the fruit of the tree" (Moses 4:18; emphasis added).

WILLINGNESS TO HEARKEN
UNTO EACH OTHER'S COUNSEL

But I think it says something very important about Adam's and Eve's relationship that she could overcome his resistance to eating the fruit: namely, we learn that Adam was willing to listen seriously to Eve and to hearken to her counsel.

Adam's decision to eat the fruit is thus an excellent example of how both husbands and wives should be willing to hearken to each other's counsel, rather than pursuing a one-sided relationship in which only one party feels obligated to listen to the other.

ADAM AND EVE BECOME SUBJECT TO DEATH AND ARE CAST OUT OF EDEN

Adam and Eve were immediately ashamed of what they had done, and attempted to cover their shame both literally, by making fig-leaf aprons to cover their nakedness, and figuratively, by hiding from the Father so they wouldn't have to confess what they had done. When the Father called to them, however, they admitted that they had eaten the forbidden fruit. In keeping with his earlier warning, the Father explained that Adam and Eve would now be subject to death. They would also have to leave the Garden and struggle through mortal existence.

> . . . Because thou hast . . . eaten of the fruit of the tree of which I commanded thee, saying Thou shalt not eat of it, cursed shall be the ground for thy sake; in sorrow shalt thou eat of it all the days of thy life.
>
> Thorns also, and thistles shall it bring forth to thee, and thou shalt eat the herb of the field.
>
> By the sweat of thy face shalt thou eat bread, until thou shalt return unto the ground for thou shalt surely die for out of it was thou taken: for dust thou wast, and unto dust shalt thou return. (Moses 4:23-25)

SATAN IS CURSED

The Father also cursed Satan for having deceived Adam and Eve. Even though Satan would have the power to cause much suffering for Adam and Eve's descendants during their mortal lives ("thou shalt bruise his heel"), he would eventually be defeated by Christ (he "shall bruise thy head"). (Genesis 3:15) The Father also reminded Satan that as a rebellious spirit, he would not be allowed to have a body; thus, even the animals were better off than he:

And I, the Lord God, said unto the serpent: Because thou hast done this thou shalt be cursed above all cattle, and above every beast of the field; upon thy belly shalt thou go, and dust shalt thou eat all the days of thy life;

And I will put enmity between thee and the woman, between thy seed and her seed; and he shall bruise thy head, and thou shalt bruise his heel. (Moses 4:20-21)

At a literal level, this curse can be read as a description of the life of a snake, since in the Genesis account it is literally a serpent which tempts Eve. In the ceremonial drama of the endowment, however, where Satan, not a serpent, appears as the tempter, these words necessarily become symbolic.

SATAN VOWS TO TEMPT MANKIND

As the ceremonial drama continues, Satan rails against God and vows to fight against man and to tempt and overcome the children of men if they don't live up to all the covenants they make in the temple ceremony. Nephi saw those temptations as an angel showed him the meaning of Lehi's vision:

The mists of darkness are the temptations of the devil, which blindeth the eyes, and hardeneth the hearts of the children of men, and leadeth them away into broad roads, that they perish and are lost. (1 Nephi 12:17)

GOD MAKES MORTALITY
A PROBATIONARY STATE

Because Adam and Eve had partaken of the fruit of the Tree of Knowledge of Good and Evil, the Father could not allow them to partake also of the Tree of Life, for then they would not have had a probationary period of mortality in which to repent of their sins. This we learn from Alma:

> And now behold, if it were possible that our first parents could have gone forth and partaken of the tree of life they would have been forever miserable, having no preparatory state; and thus the plan of redemption would have been frustrated, and the word of God would have been void, taking none effect. (Alma 12:26)

The Father and the Son therefore set cherubim to guard the way to the Tree of Life. "And the days of the children of men were prolonged, according to the will of god, that they might repent while in the flesh; wherefore, their state became a state of probation. . . ."(2 Nephi 2:21) As Amulek taught, "this life is the time for men to prepare to meet God." (Alma 34:32)

THE PROCESS OF TEACHING HOW TO
RETURN TO GOD'S PRESENCE BEGINS

The Father then began to teach Adam and Eve the signs, tokens, and key words they would need to someday return to his presence, as we learn from Joseph Smith's explanation of *Facsimile 2*, figure 3, in the *Book of Abraham*: "[God revealed] the grand Key-words of the Holy Priesthood . . . to Adam in the Garden of Eden." To gain this knowledge, of course, Adam and Eve had to first covenant to obey God's commandments.

14

THE TELESTIAL WORLD

TELESTIAL-WORLD INHABITANTS CANNOT COME TO WHERE THE FATHER AND SON DWELL

After Adam and Eve left the Garden of Eden, they were no longer able to be in the presence of either the Father or the Son. This meant that the world they lived in was telestial, since a telestial world is by definition one inhabited by people who cannot be with either the Father or the Son:

And they [the inhabitants of the telestial kingdom] shall be servants of the Most High; but where God and Christ dwell they cannot come, worlds without end. (Doctrine and Covenants 76:112)

In order to return to the Father's presence, then, Adam and Eve would need to progress beyond a telestial world. They therefore prayed to God, so they could learn what they needed to do:

> And Adam and Eve, his wife, called upon the name of the Lord, and they heard the voice of the Lord from the way toward the Garden of Eden, speaking unto them, and they saw him not; for they were shut out from his presence. (Moses 5:4)

God Sent Messengers to Teach the Plan of Salvation

After a time, the Father sent messengers to teach Adam and Eve and their descendants the plan of salvation, so they would know what to do to return to his presence. One such visitation is described in Moses 5:6-8 (when the angel appeared to Adam to explain why he had been commanded to offer sacrifice), but we learn from Alma that there were others as well:

> And after God had appointed that these things [death and judgment] should come unto man, behold, then he saw that it was expedient that man should know concerning the things whereof he had appointed unto them;
>
> Therefore he sent angels to converse with them, who caused men to behold of his glory.
>
> And they began from that time forth to call on his name; therefore God conversed with men, and made known unto them the plan of redemption, which had been prepared from the foundation of the world; and this he made known unto them according to their faith and repentance and their holy works. (Alma 12:28-30)

We learn several important things from this passage. (1) God sent messengers to teach Adam and Eve and their descendants about the judgment they would eventually have to pass to return to his presence. (More on this later.) (2) The messengers "caused men to behold of [God's] glory" which, we learn from Doctrine and Covenants 93:36, is "light and truth." (3) God revealed the plan of salvation to Adam and Eve and their descendants only as they demonstrated their faith and obedience.

SATAN ENTICED MEN TO BE CARNAL, SENSUAL, AND DEVILISH

At the same time, Satan attempted to convince Adam's and Eve's descendants that he possessed divine authority and that they should therefore listen to his teachings. Many were convinced and led astray.

> And Satan came among them [Adam's and Eve's children], saying: I am also a son of God; and he commanded them, saying [of the true teaching revealed to Adam and Eve]: Believe it not; and they believed it not, and they loved Satan more than God. And men began from that time forth to be carnal, sensual, and devilish. (Moses 5:13)

We learn in Doctrine and Covenants 46:7 that today Satan continues to try to deceive Adam's and Eve's descendants with false doctrines, which in many cases are mingled with truth so as to make them more convincing. We are warned, therefore, to be discerning, and are promised that if we look to God for guidance and keep his commandments, we will not be deceived:

But ye are commanded in all things to ask of God, who giveth liberally; and that which the Spirit testifies unto you even so I would that ye should do in all holiness of heart, walking uprightly before me, . . . that ye may not be seduced by evil spirits, or doctrines of devils, or the commandments of men; for some are of men, and others of devils.

Calling on the name of Christ, the Lord's servants in ancient times were able to command Satan to leave the faithful alone and stop trying to deceive them. See, for example, Moses's encounter with Satan (Moses 1:12-22).

THOSE WHO FAIL TO KEEP GOD'S LAWS WILL BE IN SATAN'S POWER

However, both in Adam's and Eve's time and in our own, God has warned that those who fail to keep his laws will be turned over to Satan's power, and that the Devil seeks to make them his captives. Such people will not be able to escape God's judgment:

For the kingdom of the devil must shake, and they which belong to it must needs be stirred up unto repentance, or the devil will grasp them with his everlasting chains, and they be stirred up to anger, and perish.

For behold, at that day shall he rage in the hearts of the children of men, and stir them up to anger against that which is good.

And others will he pacify, and lull them away into carnal security, that they will say: All is well in Zion; yea, Zion prospereth, all is well—and thus the devil cheateth their souls, and leadeth them away carefully down to hell.

And behold, others he flattereth away, and telleth them there is no hell; and he saith unto them: I am no devil, for there is none—and thus he whispereth in their ears, until he grasps them with his awful chains from whence there is no deliverance.

Yea, they are grasped with death, and hell; and death, and hell, and the devil, and all that have been seized therewith must stand before the throne of God, and be judged according to their works, from whence they must go into the place prepared for them, even a lake of fire and brimstone, which is endless torment.

Therefore, wo be unto him that is at ease in Zion! (2 Nephi 28:19-24)

15

THE TERRESTRIAL WORLD

TERRESTRIAL-WORLD INHABITANTS CAN BE WITH CHRIST BUT NOT THE FATHER

As Adam's and Eve's descendants follow Christ's teachings, they become worthy of living in a terrestrial world. The inhabitants of a terrestrial world are able to enjoy the Son's presence, but are still not prepared to enter the Father's presence:

> These are they who receive of the presence of the Son, but not of the fulness of the Father.
> Wherefore, they are bodies terrestrial, and bodies celestial, and differ in glory as the moon differs from the sun. (Doctrine and Covenants 76:77-78)

They still need to continue in their progression so as to be able to attain celestial glory.

OBEDIENCE TO THE LAW OF CHASTITY IS REQUIRED

The scriptures teach that to be worthy of exaltation in the celestial kingdom, people need to make and accept two significant covenants that are made at this point in the ceremonial drama: the law of chastity and the law of consecration.

The law of chastity, as explained in modern revelation, requires that people abstain from extra-marital sexual relations. Those who fail to do so, and who do not repent, will not be able to progress beyond the telestial kingdom.

> These [the inhabitants of the telestial kingdom] are they who are . . . adulterers, and whoremongers . . . (Doctrine and Covenants 76:103)

Furthermore, in order to be exalted in the highest level of the celestial kingdom, people must be married by the law of the new and everlasting covenant of marriage (Doctrine and Covenants 132:6-7). This means, of course, that they must be married and/or sealed in the temple.

> In the celestial glory there are three heavens or degrees;
> And in order to obtain the highest, a man must enter into this order of the priesthood [meaning the new and everlasting covenant of marriage];
> And if he does not, he cannot obtain it.
> He may enter into the other, but that is the end of his kingdom; he cannot have an increase. (Doctrine and Covenants 131:1-4)

WILLINGNESS TO CONSECRATE ALL FOR THE BUILDING OF ZION IS REQUIRED

From the earliest days of the Church, the Lord has commanded his Saints to "seek to bring forth and establish the cause of Zion." (Doctrine and Covenants 6:6; 11:6; 12:6; 14:6) The concept of *bringing forth Zion* seems to refer to doing missionary work; *establishing Zion* seems to refer to fulfilling our various callings in the wards and stakes of Zion.

The law of consecration, as explained in the Doctrine and Covenants, requires that members consecrate [donate, dedicate] their time, talents, and temporal goods, and all that they possess, if necessary, to the Lord for the building up of His kingdom, doing so through the agency of His Church.

As used in the scriptures, the term "Zion" refers to a specific type of society, one based on unity and righteousness. The Lord says, "Let Zion rejoice, for this is Zion—the pure in heart." (Doctrine and Covenants 97:21). Only in such a society will the Lord himself live. Since the beginning of the Restoration, Enoch's Zion has been our model:

> And from that time forth there were wars and bloodshed among them [the nations]; but the Lord came and dwelt with his people, and they dwelt in righteousness.
> . . . And the Lord called his people ZION, because they were of one heart and one mind, and dwelt in righteousness; and there was no poor among them. (Moses 7:16, 18)

TO BUILD UP ZION
IS TO BUILD OUR OWN ETERNAL HOME

The Lord makes clear that eventually, we will have to make a society like Enoch's Zion a reality here on earth, because until it is, we cannot be given a place in the celestial kingdom. Given the doctrine that this earth is to become the celestial kingdom, it seems likely that the Zion society we eventually build on earth will be the very same society in which we will live if we become heirs of the celestial kingdom. In other words, the injunction to build Zion is an injunction to build our own eternal home:

> For if you are not equal in earthly things ye cannot be equal in obtaining heavenly things;
> For if ye will that I give unto you a place in the celestial world, you must prepare yourselves by doing the things which I have commanded you and required of you. (Doctrine and Covenants 78:6-7)

Unless we as Latter-day Saints take the law of consecration seriously and work towards transforming our current societies into Zion societies, we will not be able to walk back to the presence of the Father, for the simple reason that our societies will not be of a type in which he can live with us.

Again, this building up of Zion is typically accomplished through a combination of effective missionary work and diligent service in the wards and stakes of Zion, which builds the brotherhood and love that creates a Zion society. And it is the righteousness of Zion people that lift them from a terrestrial to a celestial level.

16

A Symbolic Entry
into the
Presence of God

In the Old Testament Tabernacle,
a Veil Separated the People
from the Most Holy Place

In the Tabernacle built by Moses, the holy of holies was separated from the rest of the Tabernacle by a veil. Behind the veil was kept the ark of the covenant, where God appeared. The veil thus separated the people, including the priests officiating in the Tabernacle, from the presence of God:

And thou shalt hang up the vail under the taches, that thou mayest bring in thither within the vail the ark of the testimony: and the vail shall divide unto you between the holy place and the most holy.

And there I will meet with thee, and I will commune with thee from above the mercy seat, from between the two Cherubims which are upon the ark of the testimony, of all things which I will give thee in commandment unto the children of Israel. (Exodus 26:33; 25:22)

Only the high priest i.e., someone who had received the highest priesthood available at that time could pass through the veil, and even then only with the Lord's permission. Permission was granted every year on the Day of Atonement, when the high priest sprinkled the mercy seat with blood to atone for the people's uncleanness. At any other time, the high priest was forbidden to pass through the veil on pains of death.

And the LORD said unto Moses, Speak unto Aaron thy brother, that he come not at all times into the holy place within the vail before the mercy seat, which is upon the ark; that he die not; for I will appear in the cloud upon the mercy seat. (Leviticus 16:2)

IN THE TEMPLE, A VEIL SEPARATES THE PEOPLE FROM THE CELESTIAL ROOM

Like the Tabernacle, modern temples have a veil which separates one of the holiest areas of the temple—the celestial room—from the people participating in the ceremonial drama.

Recall Brigham Young's description of the endowment ceremony: it teaches us the signs, tokens, and key words we will need to pass the angels who stand as sentinels on the way back to God's presence. Doctrine and Covenants 132:18 also speaks of this situation, saying that "the angels and the gods are appointed there, by whom they cannot pass."

THE RICH SYMBOLISM
OF PASSING THROUGH THE VEIL

The veil symbolizes the separation between us and the presence of God. Only those who have been symbolically initiated into the highest priesthood may pass through the veil, and then only after having been symbolically granted the Lord's permission to do so. This reminds us that it is only through Christ's atonement that we are able to enter the celestial kingdom. Passing through the veil into the celestial room is a symbolic *pre-enactment* of passing the divinely appointed sentinels to enter the celestial kingdom.

Thus the veil itself, and the process of passing through the veil, is symbolic of many situations and actions. These include, (1) the mortal separation between man and God, (2) eligibility, by having been symbolically initiated into the higher priesthood, (3) eligibility, by having been given Christ's permission, through his atonement, to enter into the celestial kingdom, (4) the final judgment, and (5) possessing the required knowledge of key words, signs and tokens to be able to pass by the sentinels placed to guard the way to God's presence.

Since passing through the veil involves demonstrating one's knowledge of the essential key words and tokens, and since that process in the temple is done with the reverent coaching and assistance of temple officiators as long and as often as such assistance is needed, the veil ceremony constitutes one-on-one coaching in the most sacred things of God—a glorious blessing and individual opportunity for learning and growth!

Following the symbolic dialogue, a person representing the Lord welcomes the initiates through the veil and into the celestial room.

17

THE GLORY OF THE CELESTIAL KINGDOM

THE CELESTIAL ROOM SYMBOLIZES THE GLORY OF GOD'S PRESENCE

The Encyclopedia of Mormonism gives these fitting descriptions of the culminating area of the endowment ordinance, the celestial room:

> In the dedicatory prayer of the temple at Kirtland, Ohio, the Prophet Joseph Smith pleaded "that all people who shall enter upon the threshold of the Lord's house may feel thy power, and feel constrained to acknowledge that thou hast sanctified it, and that it is thy house, a place of thy holiness" (D&C 109:13). Of temples built by sacrifice to the name of the Lord Jesus Christ, dedicated by his authority, and reverenced in his Spirit, the promise is given, "My name shall be

here; and I will manifest myself to my people in mercy in this holy house" (D&C 110:8). In the temples there is an "aura of deity" manifest to the worthy (Kimball, pp. 534-35). Through the temple Endowment, one may seek "a fulness of the Holy Ghost" (D&C 109:15). Temple ordinances are seen as a means for receiving inspiration and instruction through the Holy Spirit, and for preparing to return to the presence of God. . . .

This order of instruction and covenant making culminates in the celestial room, which represents the highest degree of heaven, a return to the presence of God, a place of exquisite beauty and serenity, where one may feel and meditate "in the beauty of holiness" (Ps. 29:2). Communal sensitivity in the presence of like-dedicated and like-experienced loved ones enhances deep fellowship. The temple is "a house of glory" and "a place of thanksgiving for all saints" (D&C 88:119; 97:13). ("Endowment," *Encyclopedia of Mormonism*, Volume 2, p. 455 and "Temple Ordinances," Volume 4, p. 1445)

The celestial room is designed to be the most beautiful room in the temple, to symbolize the supreme glory of the Father's presence. It also symbolizes the beauty and sublimity of the eternal kingdom and city in which he dwells.

But more than that, it symbolizes the great accomplishments and rich eternal rewards of attaining exaltation in the celestial kingdom of God. Recall the glorious description of that kingdom revealed to the Prophet Joseph Smith in the great revelation describing the kingdoms of glory now known as "the vision":

And again we bear record—for we saw and heard, and this is the testimony of the gospel of Christ concerning them who shall come forth in the resurrection of the just—

They are they who received the testimony of Jesus, and believed on his name and were baptized after the manner of his burial, being buried in the water in his name, and this according to the commandment which he has given—

That by keeping the commandments they might be washed and cleansed from all their sins, and receive the Holy Spirit by the laying on of the hands of him who is ordained and sealed unto this power;

And who overcome by faith, and are sealed by the Holy Spirit of promise, which the Father sheds forth upon all those who are just and true.

They are they who are the church of the Firstborn.

They are they into whose hands the Father has given all things—

They are they who are priests and kings, who have received of his fulness, and of his glory;

And are priests of the Most High, after the order of Melchizedek, which was after the order of Enoch, which was after the order of the Only Begotten Son.

Wherefore, as it is written, they are gods, even the sons of God—

Wherefore, all things are theirs, whether life or death, or things present, or things to come, all are theirs and they are Christ's, and Christ is God's.

And they shall overcome all things.

Wherefore, let no man glory in man, but rather let him glory in God, who shall subdue all enemies under his feet.

These shall dwell in the presence of God and his Christ forever and ever.

These are they whom he shall bring with him, when he shall come in the clouds of heaven to reign on the earth over his people.

These are they who shall have part in the first resurrection.

These are they who shall come forth in the resurrection of the just.

These are they who are come unto Mount Zion, and unto the city of the living God, the heavenly place, the holiest of all.

These are they who have come to an innumerable company of angels, to the general assembly and church of Enoch, and of the Firstborn.

These are they whose names are written in heaven, where God and Christ are the judge of all.

These are they who are just men made perfect through Jesus the mediator of the new covenant, who wrought out this perfect atonement through the shedding of his own blood.

These are they whose bodies are celestial, whose glory is that of the sun, even the glory of God, the highest of all, whose glory the sun of the firmament is written of as being typical. (Doctrine and Covenants 76:50-70)

QUIET JOY AND PEACEFUL MEDITATION IN THE CELESTIAL ROOM

What a blessing it is that you may stay in the celestial room as long as you like after the endowment ceremony. Temple-goers often linger in the celestial room to pray, to reflect on personal problems, or to review in their minds what they have learned during the endowment's ceremonial drama. Also available to them, there in the celestial room, are authorized temple workers who can quietly answer questions about the endowment and other aspects of the temple when assistance is sought. They can provide further insights and understanding as you go forward in your quest for eternal truth and light.

The celestial room is a room for quiet joy and peaceful meditation. It is the place where personal revelation is often granted to those who have humbly poured out their hearts to God. It is the part of the temple where we are most likely to sense that God is there with us, as he has promised to be:

> And inasmuch as my people build a house unto me in the name of the Lord, and do not suffer any unclean thing to come into it, that it be not defiled, my glory shall rest upon it;
>
> Yea, and my presence shall be there, for I will come into it, and all the pure in heart that shall come into it shall see God. (Doctrine and Covenants 97:15-16)

Coming into the celestial room, as the final step in the endowment sequence, marks the completion of an important act of service for someone who is beyond earth life. It also marks the conclusion of an act of fervent worship and an expression of your abiding love of God:

> The privilege of entering the house of the Lord, the temple, and participating in its ordinances is a spiritual apex of LDS religious life. Through temple ordinances, one receives a ceremonial overview of and commitment to the Christlike life. Temple ordinances are instruments of spiritual rebirth. In the words of President David O. McKay, they are the "step-by-step ascent into the eternal presence." Through them, and only through them, the

powers of godliness are granted to men in the flesh (D&C 84:20-22). Temple ordinances confirm mature discipleship; they are the essence of fervent worship and an enabling and ennobling expression of one's love for God. ("Temple Ordinances," *Encyclopedia of Mormonism,* Volume 4, p. 1444)

18

LIVING THE ENDOWMENT

WITHOUT DOING TEMPLE WORK FOR OUR DEAD, WE CANNOT BE MADE PERFECT

L ike baptism, the endowment is an ordinance which is administered vicariously for the dead, so that everyone who has ever lived on earth has the opportunity to benefit from it. Performing vicarious ordinances for the dead is an extremely important work. As Joseph Smith wrote in an epistle to the saints,

> My dearly beloved—
> Let me assure you that these are principles in rela-
> tion to the dead and the living that cannot be lightly
> passed over, as pertaining to our salvation.
> For their salvation is necessary and essential to our
> salvation, as Paul says concerning the fathers—that

they without us cannot be made perfect—neither can we without our dead be made perfect. (Doctrine and Covenants 128:15)

THE PURPOSE OF THE ENDOWMENT IS TO MAKE US MORE CHRISTLIKE

Keep in mind that as far as this life is concerned, the purpose of the endowment is to make us more Christlike. God does not give us knowledge merely for its intellectual value; he expects us to use that knowledge to better serve him and our fellow human beings. The Book of Mormon reminds us that the reason God allows secret things to be made manifest, and hidden things to come to light, is so that one who receives this sacred knowledge may become "a great benefit to [his] fellow beings" (Mosiah 8:17-18).

This is a profound understanding—a guiding principle that can and should shape our lives.

If we live in keeping with the covenants we make during the endowment, we will serve others and work to make our world a more joyful, peaceful and righteous place. We will seek to bring forth and establish the cause of Zion, striving to create a Zion people within the sphere of our personal outreach. We will develop Christlike attributes and thus will feel the Spirit more powerfully in our lives, as well as help other people feel his presence in their lives.

As we work to expand our understanding of the endowment, we should give considerable attention to recognizing what we can do even better—what we can do *for others* as we strive to more fully fulfill our temple covenants. For *that*, regardless of whatever other

insights about the endowment we might receive, is ultimately what matters most.

Let us render service to both the living and to those who have gone before, for again, "we without them cannot be made perfect; neither can they without us be made perfect." (Doctrine and Covenants 128:18)

There can be no more fitting conclusion to this brief work on the symbolism of the endowment than the words Joseph Smith wrote as he concluded his glorious epistle concerning temple work, and focused on the eternal result of those who faithfully perform that work in righteousness:

> Brethren, shall we not go on in so great a cause? Go forward and not backward. Courage, brethren; and on, on to the victory! Let your hearts rejoice, and be exceedingly glad. . . . Let the dead speak forth anthems of eternal praise to the King Immanuel, who hath ordained, before the world was, that which would enable us to redeem them out of their prison; for the prisoners shall go free.
>
> . . . and let all the sons of God shout for joy! And let the eternal creations declare his name forever and ever! And again I say, how glorious is the voice we hear from heaven, proclaiming in our ears, glory, and salvation, and honor, and immortality, and eternal life; kingdoms, principalities, and powers!
>
> . . . Let us, therefore, as a church and as a people, and as Latter-day Saints, offer unto the Lord an offering in righteousness; . . . (Doctrine and Covenants 128:22-24)

WORKS CITED

The Scriptures of the Church

Book of Mormon.
Doctrine and Covenants.
Holy Bible.
Pearl of Great Price.

Other Works

Homer, Michael W. "'Similarity of Priesthood in Masonry': The Relationship between Freemasonry and Mormonism." *Dialogue,* Vol. 27, No. 3 (Fall 1993), pp. 1-113.

Ludlow, Daniel H., [ed.] *Encyclopedia of Mormonism.* 4 vols. New York: Macmillian, 1992.

Lundwall, N. B., [comp.] *Temples of the Most High.* Salt Lake City: Bookcraft, Inc., n.d.

Middlemiss, Clare, [comp.]. *Man May Know For Himself: Teachings of President David O. McKay.* Salt Lake City, Deseret Book Co., 1967.

Packer, Boyd K. *The Holy Temple.* Salt Lake City: Bookcraft, Inc., 1980.

Roberts, Brigham H., [comp.] *History of the Church.* Salt Lake City: Deseret Book Company, 1978.

Talmage, James E. *The House of the Lord.* Salt Lake City: Deseret Book Company, 1978.

Widtsoe, John A., [comp.] *Discourses of Brigham Young.* Salt Lake City: Deseret Book Company, 1941.

Widtsoe, John A. "Temple Worship," *The Utah Genealogical and Historical Magazine,* Volume 12, April 1921.

ADDITIONAL RESOURCES

(The following is a list of resources prepared either by the Church or by groups closely associated with it. You may find them useful as you prepare for the endowment or seek to deepen your appreciation of it. Some may be available in your local meetinghouse library, others from Church distribution centers, others through LDS booksellers.)

A Member's Guide to Temple and Family History Work: Ordinances and Covenants. Salt Lake City: The Church of Jesus Christ of Latter-day Saints, 1993.

Come unto Christ through Temple Ordinances. Salt Lake City: The Church of Jesus Christ of Latter-day Saints, 1987.

Hinckley, Gordon B. *Sacred Temples of the Church of Jesus Christ of Latter-day Saints.* Salt Lake City: The Church of Jesus Christ of Latter-day Saints, 1980.

——. "This Peaceful House of God." *Ensign* (May 1993), pp. 72-75.

Larsen, Dean A. "The Importance of the Temple for Living Members." *Ensign* (April 1993), p. 10-12.

Ludlow, Daniel H., ed. *Encyclopedia of Mormonism.* Vol. 4 of 5. NY: Macmillian, 1992, pp. 1444-1465.

Madsen, Truman G. *The Temple and the Atonement.* Provo: F.A.R.M.S. (Foundation for Ancient Research and Mormon Studies), 1994.

Nibley, Hugh. *The Meaning of the Temple.* Provo: F.A.R.M.S. (Foundation for Ancient Research and Mormon Studies), 1984.

Packer, Boyd K. *The Holy Temple.* Salt Lake City: Corporation of the President of The Church of Jesus Christ of Latter-day Saints, 1982.

Talmage, James E. *The House of the Lord.* Salt Lake City: Deseret Book Company, 1978.

Temples of the Ancient World: Ritual and Symbolism. Salt Lake City: Deseret Book Company, 1994.

Temples of The Church of Jesus Christ of Latter-day Saints. Salt Lake City: *Ensign* of The Church of Jesus Christ of Latter-day Saints, 1988.

Wilcox, S. Michael. *House of Glory: Finding Personal Meaning in the Temple.* Salt Lake City: Deseret Book Company, 1995.

Scripture References Cited

Doctrine and Covenants

Pearl of Great Price

INDEX

A

every gospel ordinance a covenant, 25; endowment covenants, 33-34; guide daily conduct, 34; memorize them, 35; garments remind us of, 60.
Creation—69-72.

D

Daniel—66.
David—51, 52, 53.
Death—77.
Dispensation of the fulness of times—30-31.

E

Earth—70-71.
Eden, Garden of—21; 73-79; 82.
Eloheim, Elohim—29, 70.
Endowment—a re-enactment of scriptural images and symbols, 18; Brigham Young's definition of, 19-20; covenants and promises made in, 25; modern is restoration of ancient ceremony, 27-28; tailored to specific cultures, 30-31; to meet God, 34; a gift of God's power, 43-44; empowers to return to God's presence and to receive exaltation, 45; depicts man's progression from creation to exaltation, 65; the process of teaching how to return to God's presence, 79; purpose is to make us more Christ-like, 99.
Eve—21, 59, 73-77, 79, 81-84, 87.

G

Garments—priestly, 42; modern temple garment, 55-60; garment means clothing, 55; ancient breeches to ensure modesty, 56; garments are reminders of covenants made, 60; garments are a protective shield, 60; modern resembles clothing worn by O.T. priests, 67-68; modern described, 68.
Gift of the Holy Ghost—receiving not the same as receiving the temple endowment, 44.
Gods—created the earth, 70; 72.

H

Hidden manna—63.
Holy of Holies—91.
Horizon Publishers—11-12.
Hyde, Orson—29-30.